Activities *for the* Differentiated Classroom

Gayle H. Gregory • Carolyn Chapman

CORWIN PRESS
Classroom

For information:

CORWIN PRESS

Corwin Press
A SAGE Publications Company
2455 Teller Road
Thousand Oaks, California 91320
CorwinPress.com

SAGE, Ltd.
1 Oliver's Yard
55 City Road
London EC1Y 1SP
United Kingdom

SAGE India Pvt. Ltd.
B 1/I 1 Mohan Cooperative
Industrial Area
Mathura Road, New Delhi
India 110 044

SAGE Asia-Pacific Pvt. Ltd.
33 Pekin Street #02-01
Far East Square
Singapore 048763

Printed in the United States of America.

ISBN 978-1-4129-5336-8

This book is printed on acid-free paper.

08 09 10 11 12 10 9 8 7 6 5 4 3 2 1

Executive Editor: Kathleen Hex
Managing Developmental Editor: Christine Hood
Editorial Assistant: Anne O'Dell
Developmental Writer: Jeanine Manfro
Developmental Editor: Kathleen Hex
Proofreader: Bette Darwin
Art Director: Anthony D. Paular
Cover Designer: Monique Hahn
Interior Production Artist: Lisa Riley

Activities for the
Differentiated
Classroom

GRADE K

TABLE OF CONTENTS

Connections to Standards

This chart shows the national academic standards covered in each chapter.

MATHEMATICS	Standards are covered on pages
Numbers and Operations—Understand numbers, ways of representing numbers, relationships among numbers, and number systems.	9, 12
Algebra—Understand patterns, relations, and functions.	15
Geometry—Analyze characteristics and properties of two- and three-dimensional geometric shapes, and develop mathematical arguments about geometric relationships.	16
Measurement—Understand measurable attributes of objects and the units, systems, and processes of measurement.	19, 22
Measurement—Apply appropriate techniques, tools, and formulas to determine measurements.	22
Data Analysis and Probability—Formulate questions that can be addressed with data, and collect, organize, and display relevant data to answer them.	25

SCIENCE	Standards are covered on pages
Science as Inquiry—Ability to conduct scientific inquiry.	34
Physical Science—Understand properties of objects and materials.	28, 31, 37
Physical Science—Understand light, heat, electricity, and magnetism.	34
Life Science—Understand characteristics of organisms.	40, 43, 45
Life Science—Understand organisms and environments.	43
Earth and Space Science—Understand properties of earth materials.	49
Earth and Space Science—Understand changes in the earth and sky.	52

SOCIAL STUDIES	Standards are covered on pages
Understand the interactions among people, places, and environments.	56, 63
Understand individual development and identity.	63
Understand interactions among individuals, groups, and institutions.	56
Understand how people create and change structures of power, authority, and governance.	67
Understand how people organize for the production, distribution, and consumption of goods and services.	60

Understand relationships among science, technology, and society.	60
Understand the ideals, principles, and practices of citizenship in a democratic republic.	67

LANGUAGE ARTS	Standards are covered on pages
Read a wide range of print and nonprint texts to build an understanding of texts, of self, and of the cultures of the United States and the world; to acquire new information; to respond to the needs and demands of society and the workplace; and for personal fulfillment (includes fiction and nonfiction, classic, and contemporary works).	87
Read a wide range of literature from many periods in many genres to build an understanding of the many dimensions (e.g., philosophical, ethical, aesthetic) of human experience.	87
Apply a wide range of strategies to comprehend, interpret, evaluate, and appreciate texts. Draw on prior experience, interactions with other readers and writers, knowledge of word meaning and of other texts, word identification strategies, and understanding of textual features (e.g., sound-letter correspondence, sentence structure, context, graphics).	69, 71, 74, 77, 80, 84
Adjust the use of spoken, written, and visual language (e.g., conventions, style, vocabulary) to communicate effectively with a variety of audiences and for different purposes.	84, 90
Apply knowledge of language structure, language conventions (e.g., spelling and punctuation), media techniques, figurative language, and genre to create, critique, and discuss print and nonprint texts.	71, 84, 90

Introduction

As a teacher who has adopted the differentiated philosophy, you design instruction to embrace the diversity of the unique students in your classroom and strategically select tools to build a classroom where all students can succeed. This requires careful planning and a very large toolkit! You must make decisions about what strategies and activities best meet the needs of the students in your classroom at that time. It is not a "one size fits all" approach.

When planning for differentiated instruction, include the steps described below. Refer to the planning model in *Differentiated Instructional Strategies: One Size Doesn't Fit All, Second Edition* (Gregory & Chapman, 2007) for more detailed information.

1. Establish standards, essential questions, and expectations for the lesson or unit.

2. Identify content, including facts, vocabulary, and essential skills.

3. Activate prior knowledge. Preassess students' levels of readiness for the learning and collect data on students' interests and attitudes about the topic.

4. Determine what students need to learn and how they will learn it. Plan various activities that complement the learning styles and readiness levels of all students in this particular class. Locate appropriate resources or materials for all levels of readiness.

5. Apply the strategies and adjust to meet students' varied needs.

6. Decide how you will assess students' knowledge. Consider providing choices for students to demonstrate what they know.

Differentiation does not mean always tiering every lesson for three levels of complexity or challenge. It does mean finding interesting, engaging, and appropriate ways to help students learn new concepts and skills. The practical activities in this book are designed to support your differentiated lesson plans. They are not prepackaged units but rather activities you can incorporate into your plan for meeting the unique needs of the students in your classroom right now. Use these activities as they fit into differentiated lessons or units you are planning. They might be used for total group lessons, to reinforce learning with individuals or small groups, to focus attention, to provide additional rehearsal opportunities, or to assess knowledge. Your differentiated toolkit should be brimming with engaging learning opportunities. Take out those tools and start building success for all your students!

Put It into Practice

Differentiation is a Philosophy

For years teachers planned "the lesson" and taught it to all students, knowing that some will get it and some will not. Faced with NCLB and armed with brain research, we now know that this method of lesson planning will not reach the needs of all students. Every student learns differently. In order to leave no child behind, we must teach differently.

Differentiation is a philosophy that enables teachers to plan strategically in order to reach the needs of the diverse learners in the classroom and to help them meet the standards. Supporters of differentiation as a philosophy believe:

- All students have areas of strength.

- All students have areas that need to be strengthened.

- Each student's brain is as unique as a fingerprint.

- It is never too late to learn.

- When beginning a new topic, students bring their prior knowledge base and experience to the new learning.

- Emotions, feelings, and attitudes affect learning.

- All students can learn.

- Students learn in different ways at different times.

The Differentiated Classroom

A differentiated classroom is one in which the teacher responds to the unique needs of the students in that room, at that time. Differentiated instruction provides a variety of options to successfully reach targeted standards. It meets learners where they are and offers challenging, appropriate options for them to achieve success.

Differentiating Content By differentiating content the standards are met while the needs of the particular students being taught are considered. The teacher strategically selects the information to teach and the best resources with which to teach it using different genres, leveling materials, using a variety of instructional materials, and providing choice.

Differentiating Assessment Tools Most teachers already differentiate assessment during and after the learning. However, it is equally important to assess what knowledge or interests students bring to the learning formally or informally.

Assessing student knowledge prior to the learning experience helps the teacher find out:

- What standards, objectives, concepts, skills the students already understand

- What further instruction and opportunities for mastery are needed

- What areas of interests and feelings will influence the topic under study

- How to establish flexible groups—total, alone, partner, small group

Differentiating Performance Tasks In a differentiated classroom, the teacher provides various opportunities and choices for the students to show what they've learned. Students use their strengths to show what they know through a reflection activity, a portfolio, or an authentic task.

Differentiating Instructional Strategies When teachers vary instructional strategies and activities, more students learn content and meet standards. By targeting diverse intelligences and learning styles, teachers can develop learning activities that help students work in their areas of strength as well as areas that still need strengthening.

Some of these instructional strategies include:

- Graphic organizers

- Cubing

- Role-playing

- Centers

- Choice boards

- Adjustable assignments

- Projects

- Academic contracts

When planning, teachers in the differentiated classroom focus on the standards, but also adjust and redesign the learning activities, tailoring them to the needs of the unique learners in each classroom. Teachers also consider how the brain operates and strive to use research-based, best practices to maximize student learning. Through differentiation we give students the opportunity to learn to their full potential. A differentiated classroom engages students and facilitates learning so all learners can succeed!

CHAPTER 1

Mathematics

Number Lineup

Standard

Numbers and Operations—Understand numbers, ways of representing numbers, relationships among numbers, and number systems.

Objective

Students will count objects and place numbers in order.

Materials

Number Lineup reproducible
plastic sandwich bags
various small items (cotton balls, paper clips, marbles)
paper lunch bags

Strategy
Cooperative group learning

Students in kindergarten need to develop a clear concept of what numbers are. Counting objects and placing numbers in order are important skills that will help develop this concept. This activity provides practice in counting and ordering numbers while allowing students to work together in small groups.

1. Prepare a set of counting bags for each group of students. To make the bags, fill 30 plastic sandwich bags with various items. Use small items such as cotton balls, crayons, paper clips, and coins. Place one item in the first bag, two items in the second bag, three items in the third bag, and so on until the last bag has 30 items. Place all 30 bags into a paper lunch bag to keep the set together.

2. Introduce the lesson by having students recite the nursery rhyme "One, Two, Buckle My Shoe." Talk about the numbers in the nursery rhyme, and have student volunteers find items around the classroom that represent each number from 1 to 10. Then, as a group, count aloud from 1 to 30.

3. After preassessing students' counting readiness, divide the class into mixed-ability groups of four. Distribute the counting bags that were assembled in Step 1 to each group. Have students work together to count the items in each bag. Then have them place the

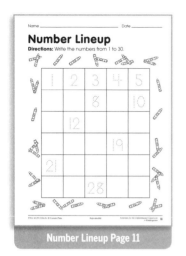

bags in order, starting with the bag containing one item. Finally, have the students arrange the items in rows to show the numbers from 1 to 30.

◄ 4. Give students who are ready a copy of the **Number Lineup reproducible (page 11)**. Have students practice writing the numbers 1 to 30 in order on the page. Beginning mastery students can work at tracing number manipulatives on a magnetic board with their fingers.

Ideas for More Differentiation

Have students with a high degree of mastery use the counting bags for numbers 1 to 10 to create simple addition problems. For example, they can use the bag with two items and the bag with three items to demonstrate that 2 + 3 = 5.

Number Lineup

Directions: Write the numbers from 1 to 30.

1	2	3	4	5
		8		10
	12			
			19	
21				
		28		

More or Less

Standard

Numbers and Operations—Understand numbers, ways of representing numbers, relationships among numbers, and number systems.

Objective

Students will identify *more than, less than,* and *equal to.*

Materials

More or Less reproducible

multiple objects of varying sizes (2 tennis balls, 2 basketballs)

An important part of understanding numbers is differentiating between varying quantities. Students need practice in comparing sets of items and identifying which set has more items, which set has fewer items, and which sets have an equal number of items. At the kindergarten level, some students will mistakenly assume that a set of large objects will automatically contain more items than a set of small objects. This activity will help students to use the number, rather than the size of objects to determine *more than, less than,* and *equal to.*

1. Collect sets of objects that represent various numbers. For example, gather 2 tennis balls and 5 tennis balls, 15 pencils and 12 pencils, 30 cotton swabs and 10 cotton swabs, 6 oranges and 8 oranges, and so on. Collect another group of sets that have items of varying sizes. For example, use 2 beach balls and 8 golf balls, 21 crayons and 11 erasers, 17 pairs of scissors and 11 brads, 4 sheets of paper and 4 paper clips, and so on.

2. Introduce or review the phrases *more than, less than,* and *equal to to.* Have students describe each phrase and demonstrate their understanding by organizing the sets into groups containing different-sized objects. Ask questions that will help students identify which group has more items and which has fewer.

3. Show the students two sets of objects that feature different-sized items, such as the beach balls and golf balls. Ask: *Which set has more?* Point out that the beach balls are larger than the golf balls but that there are more golf balls than beach balls.

4. Place all the sets on a table, and invite student pairs to investigate them. Have them count the objects in each pair of sets and determine which set has more, which has fewer, and which are equal. Observe students to assess their level of mastery.

5. Give each student a copy of the **More or Less reproducible (page 14)**. Have students use rubber stamps and an ink pad to stamp sets of pictures to represent the concepts of *more*, *less*, and *equal to*.

6. Assess each student's level of mastery for determining *more than*, *less than*, and *equal to*. Continue the learning in a way that meets the needs of students at all levels.

▶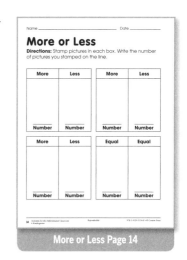

More or Less Page 14

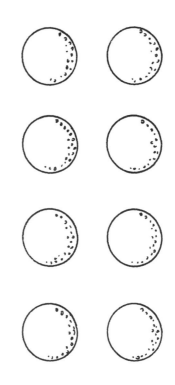

More or Less

Directions: Stamp pictures in each box. Write the number of pictures you stamped on the line.

More	Less
_____	**_____**
Number	**Number**

More	Less
_____	**_____**
Number	**Number**

More	Less
_____	**_____**
Number	**Number**

Equal	Equal
_____	**_____**
Number	**Number**

978-1-4129-5336-8 • © Corwin Press

Sort It Out

Standard
Algebra—Understand patterns, relations, and functions.

Objective
Students will sort and classify objects.

Materials
2 hula-hoops
large box

Sorting and classifying objects by attributes is an important skill that begins the process of algebraic thinking. In Sort It Out, students will sort and classify various objects based on their attributes.

1. The day before this lesson, divide the class into three groups. Ask the first group to bring something from home that is yellow. Ask the second group to bring something blue. And ask the third group to bring something that is both yellow and blue. You may wish to send reminder notes home asking parents to label the items with the student's name.

2. Tape two hula-hoops together so they form a Venn-diagram shape.

3. On the day of the lesson, collect the items that were brought from home in a single box. Show students the collection of items in the box. Display the hoops on the floor or a table. Tell students that they are going to sort the items by color. Indicate that one hoop will be for the yellow items, one hoop will be for the blue items, and the overlapping part in the middle will be for the yellow and blue items.

4. Display one item from the box at a time. Let the student who brought the item place it in the appropriate section of the hoops. Continue until all the items have been placed. Close the activity by reviewing what the class accomplished.

Extend the Activity
Invite students to think of ways to sort other objects from around the room, such as things that are square, things that are hard, and things that are hard and square. Provide plenty of time for students to practice defining attributes, finding things that match those attributes, using the hoops to sort them.

Searching for Shapes

Strategy
Rehearsal

Standard

Geometry—Analyze characteristics and properties of two- and three-dimensional geometric shapes, and develop mathematical arguments about geometric relationships.

Objective

Students will identify geometric shapes in everyday objects and discuss the characteristics of the shapes with a partner.

Materials

Searching for Shapes reproducible
construction paper
scissors
glue

In this activity, students use what they have learned about shapes. Finding geometric shapes within everyday objects will help students improve their understanding of the characteristics and properties of shapes. They will then demonstrate their knowledge by creating a picture of a common object using the geometric shapes.

1. Prior to the activity, cut squares, rectangles, triangles, and circles from different-colored construction paper. Include various sizes for each shape. Put the shapes in a box, and set them aside to use later.

2. Review with the students the features of four basic geometric shapes—square, rectangle, triangle, and circle. Show each shape, and describe its characteristics and properties.

3. Give students a copy of the **Searching for Shapes reproducible (page 18)**, and invite them to go on a scavenger hunt for shapes around the classroom. Tell students to look for squares, rectangles, triangles, and circles in everyday objects around the room. For example, the classroom clock is the shape of a circle, and a bookcase is the shape of a rectangle. As students identify shapes, have them draw on the reproducible pictures of the objects that have those shapes.

Searching for Shapes Page 18

4. Gather the students back together in a group. Ask them to share with a partner what they found and recorded on their papers. Remind them to describe the characteristics of the shapes as they discuss them. Invite volunteers to share their work with the group.

5. Give each student a large sheet of construction paper. Have students use the paper shapes from Step 1 to design a picture of an everyday object that uses one or more of the shapes. Let them glue the shapes to the construction paper to make a picture.

Ideas for More Differentiation

For students at the beginning mastery level, select one shape to focus on, and have the students make a collage using only that shape. Provide construction paper in a variety of colors and have students cut the shape from several different colors of paper. Then encourage them to arrange the shapes on another sheet of paper and glue them in place.

Name _____ Date _____

Searching for Shapes

Directions: Draw pictures of things that have these shapes.

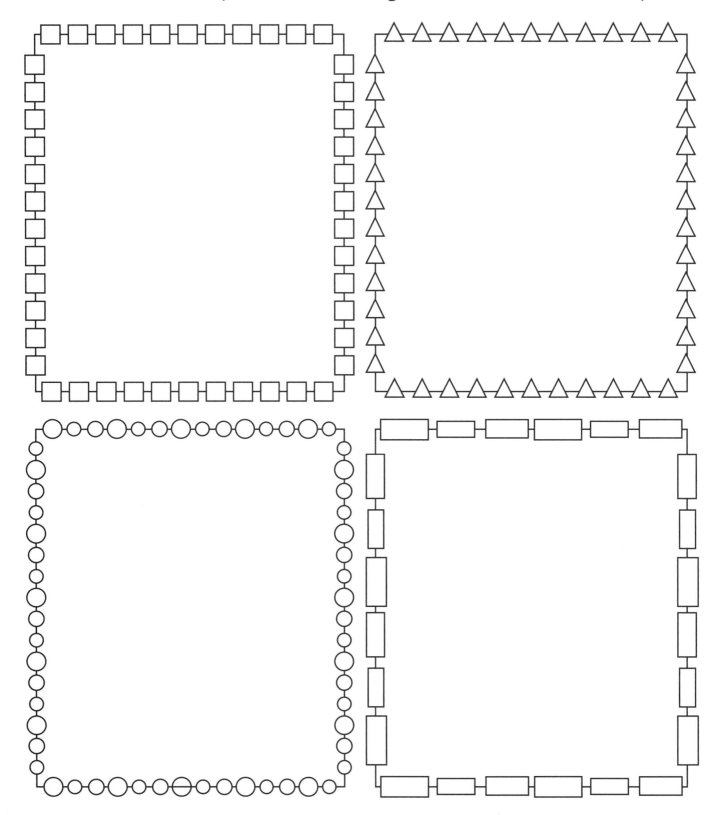

     978-1-4129-5336-8 • © Corwin Press

Time for a Talk

Standard
Measurement—Understand measurable attributes of objects and the units, systems, and processes of measurement.

Objective
Students will identify times of day and how they relate to familiar events.

Materials
Time for a Talk reproducible
classroom learning clock

Strategies
Rehearsal

Presentation

This activity will help beginning mastery students think about how time relates to the events that happen throughout the day. Through classroom presentations, students will have the opportunity to practice speaking and listening, putting events in order, and using a clock to tell time.

1. Use a classroom learning clock to review with students the concept of telling time. Show students the clock's hands and how they rotate around as time progresses. Place the minute hand at *12* and the hour hand at *3* to demonstrate the time *3:00*. Invite student volunteers to demonstrate how the hour hand moves around the clock for each new hour. Continue the discussion by highlighting certain times of day. For example, show the time as 3:00. Ask students what they are usually doing at three o'clock. Do the same for other times of day.

2. Give each student a copy of **Time for a Talk reproducible (page 21)**. Tell students to use the page to organize their thoughts about things they do throughout the day. Invite them to draw pictures in each section to show morning activities, afternoon activities, and evening activities.

3. After students finish drawing, instruct them to circle one illustrated event in each section. Ask students to think about a specific time of day (to the nearest hour) when each circled event occurs. Then have them draw hands on the clock next to the section to indicate the time and write the time next to the clock. For example, eating breakfast might occur at 7:00 in the morning. The clock next to the morning section would have hands indicating 7:00, and *7:00* would be written on the line next to the clock.

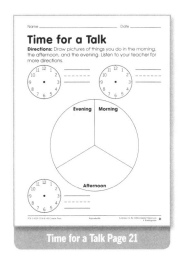

Time for a Talk Page 21

4. Let each student give a brief presentation to the group. Have the student use his or her paper and the classroom learning clock as visual aids. Each student will identify an activity for the morning, the afternoon, and the evening and use the clock to show when the activities take place. For example, a student might say: *I eat breakfast at 7:00. I go to soccer practice at 3:00. I take a bath at 6:00.*

Ideas for More Differentiation

Have students interview their parents to find out about their daily schedules. Have students make posters to show the times when their parents do certain activities.

Name _____ Date _____

Time for a Talk

Directions: Draw pictures of things you do in the morning, the afternoon, and the evening. Listen to your teacher for more directions.

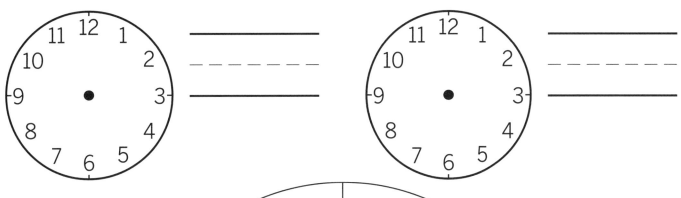

_____
- - - - - - - - - - - - - - -
_____

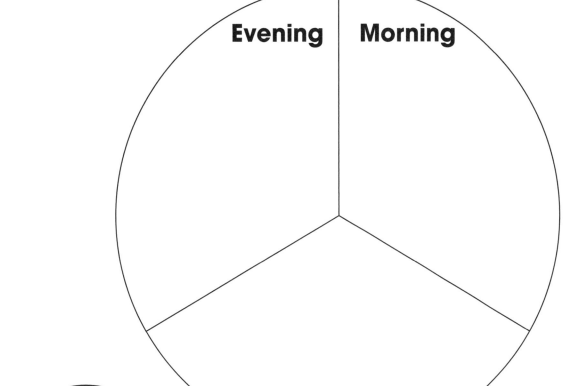

Evening   Morning

Afternoon

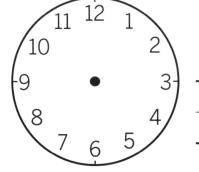

_____
- - - - - - - - - - - - - - -
_____

Measure Up

Standards

Measurement—Understand measurable attributes of objects and the units, systems, and processes of measurement.
Apply appropriate techniques, tools, and formulas to determine measurements.

Objective

Students will measure a variety of objects using the appropriate tools.

Materials

Measure Up reproducible
various classroom objects for measuring
balance scale
construction paper
stapler

In this activity, students will have the opportunity to compare the length, weight, and capacity of different objects.

Measure Up Page 24

1. Make a copy of the **Measure Up reproducible (page 24)** for each student. Fold a large sheet of construction paper in half to make a folder and staple the reproducible to the front of the folder.

2. Gather students into a group, and have the tallest student stand next to the shortest student. Compare their heights, and discuss different methods that could be used to measure the students (paperclip chains, stacks of books, measuring tape, etc.).

3. Collect several objects from around the room, and demonstrate ways of measuring the objects' lengths. Show students how to measure capacity by filling different-sized containers with various objects and making comparisons between them. Finally, use a balance scale to show students how to compare the weights of two objects.

4. Distribute the folders made in Step 1. Read through the reproducible instructions with students. Determine if you want students to work alone, in pairs, or as a whole group.

5. Allow each student to choose the activities from the reproducible that he or she would like to complete. Have students draw a picture on a sheet of construction paper to show what they learned from each activity, and place the pictures in the folder. Be sure to have students mark the box for each activity completed.

6. When students have completed all of the chosen activities, staple their pictures together inside the construction paper folder to make a measurement book. If you like, have students write or dictate a sentence describing each picture.

Ideas for More Differentiation

If you decide to group students, do so based on their level of readiness for learning about measurement. Think about using mixed-ability grouping for the benefit of all students.

Name _____ Date _____

Measure Up

Directions: Pick a box, and follow the instructions inside it. Draw a picture to show what you learned.

1. Pick a 🪑. Use your ✋ to measure how long it is.	**2.** Pick ✏️. Use ⛓️ to measure how long each one is.
3. Get a 🍵 and a 🥣. Fill them with 🫘. Count to see which one holds more.	**4.** Get a 🪣 and a 🧺. Fill both with 🧱. Count to see which one holds more.
5. Pick 📚. Use a ⚖️ to see which is heaviest.	**6.** Pick ⚽⚽. Use a ⚖️ to see which is heaviest.

978-1-4129-5336-8 • © Corwin Press

Graphs Galore

Standard
Data Analysis and Probability—Formulate questions that can be addressed with data, and collect, organize, and display relevant data to answer them.

Strategy
Cooperative group learning

Objective
Students will collect, organize, and display data relevant to a self-selected question.

Materials
Graphs Galore reproducible
yarn
poster board
stapler
sticky notes
crayons or markers

In this activity, students work in cooperative groups to create a graph. Throughout the project, students practice skills in data collection and analysisand the communication of mathematical ideas.

1. After preassessing learning readiness and surveying learning styles, divide the class into groups of four. Consider mixing learning styles and readiness levels. Help each group decide on a question to use for a graph, such as: *How many children live in your house? What is your favorite fruit? What is your favorite color? What is your favorite nursery rhyme?*

2. Give each group a sheet of poster board and a skein of yarn. Write the group's question along the top of the poster board. Then have students cut and measure lengths of yarn to make rows and columns on the poster board. Help students staple the lengths of yarn in place.

3. Direct each group to provide choices on its graph. For example, if the question is *What is your favorite fruit?*, students in that group should select four or five fruits and draw pictures of them along the top row of the graph.

4. Staple the graphs along a wall. Give students several sticky notes. Have them write their names on the notes and attach one note to each graph to indicate their answers.

5. Ask the groups to present their graphs to the class. Have the students in each group explain different concepts illustrated by the graph. For example, if the group made a Favorite Fruit Graph, one student might identify which fruit got the most votes, and another student might identify which one got the fewest.

6. Give each student a copy of the **Graphs Galore reproducible (page 27)**. Read each statement to the students, and have them circle *Yes* or *No* to indicate their level of participation in the project.

Ideas for More Differentiation

Encourage students with a high degree of mastery to interview students in other classrooms to expand on the data for their graphs. Have them compare the data between different groups.

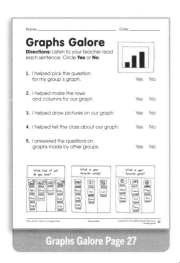

Graphs Galore Page 27

Graphs Galore

Directions: Listen to your teacher read each sentence. Circle **Yes** or **No**.

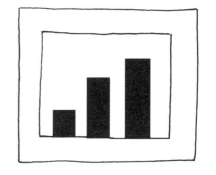

1. I helped pick the question for my group's graph.   Yes   No

2. I helped make the rows and columns for our graph.   Yes   No

3. I helped draw pictures on our graph.   Yes   No

4. I helped tell the class about our graph.   Yes   No

5. I answered the questions on graphs made by other groups.   Yes   No

Come to Your Senses

Standard

Physical Science—Understand properties of objects and materials.

Objective

Students will investigate the physical properties of objects and complete a graphic organizer to classify the objects by defined attributes.

Materials

Come to Your Senses reproducible
objects to engage the five senses
boxes to hold objects

Learning about the five senses gives students the opportunity to explore and describe things within their own environment. In this activity, students investigate the physical properties of objects. They will then use a graphic organizer to classify the objects by defined attributes.

1. Prepare five stations for investigating objects by using the senses. Collect objects that can be classified as follows: sight—shiny, dull, colorful, and transparent; smell—sweet, sharp, flowery, minty; sound—loud, quiet, high, low; touch—hard, soft, rough, smooth; taste—sweet, sour, salty, bitter. For taste and smell, be sure to avoid itams that might trigger allergic reactions. Place a box at each station to hold the collected objects.

2. Preassess students' level of readiness for learning about the senses, sorting and classifying objects, and identifying physical properties of objects.

3. Divide the class into five mixed-ability groups. Send each group to a separate station. Allow the groups to investigate the objects, and have them sort them into categories of their own choosing. Have the groups rotate through the stations so that each group has time to explore each of the five senses. After each rotation, restock the smell and taste stations so the samples are fresh.

4. Gather the class together, and ask volunteers how they sorted items at each station. Then explain the categories listed in Step 1 and have groups go back through each station and sort the items by those categories. Give each group five copies of the **Come to Your Senses reproducible (page 30)**. For each station, model how to write the name of the sense in the center rectangle and a different category in each of the connected rectangles. (You may wish to provide prepared reproducibles depending on students' skill levels.) As students sort the items, have them take turns drawing pictures or writing the names of the objects in the appropriate boxes on each page.

▶

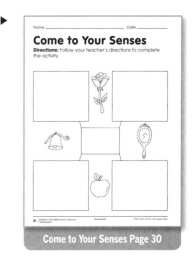

Come to Your Senses Page 30

5. Bring the class together once again. Invite volunteers to share their learning. Encourage students to reflect on their learning by drawing or writing in their journals.

Come to Your Senses

Directions: Follow your teacher's directions to complete the activity.

978-1-4129-5336-8 • © Corwin Press

Float or Sink

Standard
Physical Science—Understand properties of objects and materials.

Objective
Students will experiment to discover what will float and what will sink. They will then assemble a floating boat and a sinking sub.

Materials
Float or Sink reproducible
plastic tubs
water
objects that float
objects that sink

In this activity, students will experiment with different types of material to see what will float in water and what will sink. Students will then assemble different materials to make a floating boat and a sinking sub.

1. Begin by activating students' prior knowledge. Show students pictures of boats and submarines. Ask them to describe the differences and similarities between different types of vessels.

2. Set out tubs of water and a variety of materials, some of which will sink in water and some of which will float. Here are some suggestions for the materials:
   - wooden blocks
   - sponges
   - empty plastic bottles
   - rubber balls
   - pencils
   - unwrapped crayons
   - straws
   - coins
   - balls of clay
   - metal washers
   - sealed sandwich bags filled with sand
   - magnets
   - apples
   - oranges
   - corks

Float or Sink Page 33

3. Give each student a copy of the **Float or Sink reproducible (page 33)**. Let students experiment with the items listed in Step 2, testing which items sink and which float. Have students record their observations on the reproducible.

4. Let each student use some of the materials from Step 2 to build a boat and a submarine. Have students use multiple materials for each vessel. You may wish to encourage them to try combining floating and sinking materials to make one vessel. Have students draw pictures of their boats and submarines on the reproducible.

Ideas for More Differentiation

Ask students with a high degree of mastery to experiment with the weight of objects. Have them construct submarines of different weights. Then use a stopwatch to time how quickly each submarine sinks to the bottom of the tub. Encourage students to guess why some submarines sink faster than others.

Name _____ Date _____

Float or Sink

Directions: Draw pictures of things that float. Draw pictures of things that sink.

Float	**Sink**

Directions: Draw pictures of the boat and sub you made.

My Boat	**My Sub**

Stick To It

Strategies

Cooperative group learning

Authentic task

Standards

Science as Inquiry—Ability to conduct scientific inquiry.
Physical Science—Understand light, heat, electricity, and magnetism.

Objective

Students will conduct a scientific inquiry to learn about magnets.

Materials

Stick To It reproducible
magnets of different strengths and sizes
paper clips

Asking questions, making predictions, and conducting experiments are important to learning about science. In this activity, students will conduct a scientific inquiry to learn about magnets. They will discover that not all magnets have the same strength and that larger magnets are not necessarily stronger than smaller magnets.

1. Prior to the activity, gather a collection of magnets. Include those with different shapes, sizes, and strengths. Place a small sticker on each magnet, and number them for record-keeping purposes.

2. Help students activate prior knowledge about magnets. Guide a class discussion. Display the magnets, and ask questions such as: *What do magnets do? Which magnet do you think is the strongest? Which do you think is the weakest? How can we find out?*

3. Divide the class into five cooperative groups. Give each group two magnets, a box of paper clips, and a copy of the **Stick To It reproducible (page 36)**. Have the students predict which of their two magnets is the strongest and write its number on the reproducible. Then, have them predict how many paper clips the magnet will hold end-to-end and record the number. Have them repeat this procedure with the second magnet.

4. Now let students check their predictions. Have them place paper clips end-to-end on each of their magnets. Then ask them to count the total number on each magnet and record the results on their reproducible.

5. Have groups trade pairs of magnets and continue the experiment until each group has worked with each pair of magnets.

6. After the experiments are complete, collect all the magnets, and gather the class together. Prepare a simple bar graph for each numbered magnet. Have one student from each group draw an X on the graph for every paper clip that the magnet held. Compare the results of the different graphs to determine which magnet was strongest and which was weakest.

Stick To It Page 36

Stick To It

Directions: Which magnet do you think will be strongest? Write its number in the first column. Predict how many paper clips it will hold. Write that number next. Test your prediction. How many paper clips did the magnet hold? Write your answer in the last column.

Magnet Number	Our Prediction	Our Results

Wonderful Water

Standard
Physical Science—Understand properties of objects and materials.

Objective
Students will observe the three forms of water—liquid, solid, and gas.

Materials
Wonderful Water reproducible
water
glass containers of various sizes and shapes
tea kettle
heating element
mirror
ice block
chart paper
marker

Kindergarten students may think of water only in its liquid form. In this focus activity, students will begin to discover the three forms of water—liquid, solid, and gas. They will also observe that water can be changed from one form to another and back again.

1. Create a K-W-L chart about water with your students. Divide a sheet of chart paper into three columns. Label the first column *K* for *know*, the second *W* for *want to know*, and the third *L* for *learned*. Ask students questions such as: *What do you know about water? What shape does it have? What does it smell like, taste like, and feel like? Is it always a liquid?* Record students' responses on the chart under the *K*. Then ask them what they want to learn about water, and record those responses on the chart under the *W*.

2. Boil some water in a tea kettle or other container, and let students observe the steam rising up from the kettle. Explain that steam is the result of changing liquid water into a vapor or gas. Hold a mirror over the steam, and allow students to observe the condensation that forms. Discuss how this is an example of steam changing back into a liquid.

3. Now display a block of ice and a glass of water. Pour the water from the glass into another container so students can observe how the water moves and changes shape to fit its container. Ask students how they could change the water into ice and the ice into water. Then ask them how the ice and the water could each be changed into steam.

4. Complete the K-W-L chart from Step 1 by asking students what they have learned about water. Record their responses on the chart. Then give each student a copy of the **Wonderful Water reproducible (page 39)**. Have students color the pictures, cut out the boxes, and staple the minibook together.

Ideas for More Differentiation

Instruct students with a high degree of mastery to design posters about how water in all its forms is used in everyday life. Have individual students give presentations to the class about water conservation.

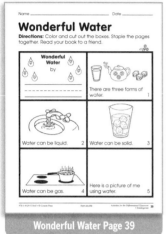

Wonderful Water Page 39

Wonderful Water

Directions: Color and cut out the boxes. Staple the pages together. Read your book to a friend.

Wonderful Water

by

_____
_ _ _ _ _ _ _ _ _ _ _ _ _ _
_____

There are three forms of water.   1

Water can be liquid.   2

Water can be solid.   3

Water can be gas.   4

Here is a picture of me using water.   5

Plentiful Plants

Standard

Life Science—Understand characteristics of organisms.

Objective

Students will develop observational skills and learn about the basic structures of plants.

Materials

Plentiful Plants reproducible
potted plants
magnifying glasses

In this activity, students develop their observational skills and increase their vocabularies as they compare different plants. They will also learn about the basic structure of plants.

1. Prior to this lesson, ask parents to donate small, inexpensive potted plants to the classroom. Be sure to tell parents that the plants will not be returned to them. Bring a few plants for those students who are not able to donate their own.

2. Preassess students' readiness for learning about plant parts.

3. Create a center for observing the plants. Provide small magnifying glasses for students to use. Show them the three parts of the center. Guide students to complete the activity or activities that best suit their level of readiness.

4. **Sorting:** Encourage students to study the plants carefully and use their characteristic to group them into by leaf shape, color, size, type of stem, etc. Ask individuals or small groups to share the ways in which they grouped the plants.

5. **Comparison:** Provide numerous copies of the **Plentiful Plants reproducible (page 42)**. Have students visit the plant center and select two plants to compare. Tell them to record their observations on the reproducible.

Plentiful Plants Page 42

6. **Physical Investigation:** Allow students to choose one plant from the center for further investigation. Let students take the plant out of the pot to study its root system. Ask them to point out the roots, stem, leaves, and flowers on the plants, and ask students to discuss the purpose of each structure. Guide the students into understanding that roots usually go down into the soil and are used for getting nutrients out of the soil, that stems are the main support for the plant and usually they grow up out of the soil, that leaves are usually attached to the stem and are often colored green, and that flowers produce seeds and are sometimes colorful.

7. Ask students to share with a partner what they learned about plants. Encourage them to show their partner the results of their work. After everyone has visited the center, invite volunteers to share with the whole class.

Plentiful Plants

Directions: Choose two plants. Draw a picture of each one.

Directions: Circle three things on the plants that are the same. Draw a box around three things that are different. Write about how the plants are alike and different.

The plants are alike because _____

_____

The plants are different because _____

_____

978-1-4129-5336-8 • © Corwin Press

Amazing Animals

Standards
Life Science—Understand characteristics of organisms.
Understand organisms and environments.

Objective
Students will classify animals.

Materials
Amazing Animals reproducible
toy animals
music CD or cassette
CD or cassette player

Strategy
Preassessment

Young children are naturally fascinated by animals. They like to learn about how animals move, sound, and live. With this activity, you can capitalize on your students' interest in animals and assess their level of readiness for classifying animals.

1. Capture your students' attention with a brief focus activity. Play some instrumental music, and tell students to stand up. Then call out the name of an animal such as *elephant, cow, lion,* or *fish,* and encourage students to imitate the sounds and movements of the given animal. Continue with several different animals, or let one student at a time name the animal to be imitated.

2. Set out a collection of small toy animals. Include a large variety of both domestic and wild animals. Be sure to have mammals, reptiles, birds, insects, and fish represented.

3. Ask students to suggest ways to sort the animals. Some possible classifications include number of legs, type of body covering, type of food they eat, places they live, types of sounds they make, and ways they move. Create a word list from the suggestions.

4. Make several copies of the **Amazing Animals reproducible (page 44)** for each student. Place the reproducibles, the word list, and the toy animal collection in a center. Allow students to visit the center individually or in pairs to sort and classify the animals in different ways. Have students record their classifications on a reproducible.

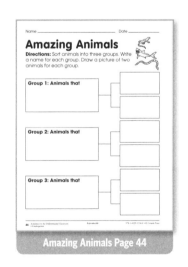

Amazing Animals Page 44

Name _____ Date _____

Amazing Animals

Directions: Sort animals into three groups. Write a name for each group. Draw a picture of two animals for each group.

Group 1: Animals that

Group 2: Animals that

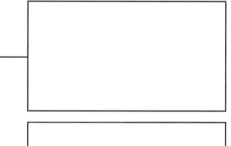

Group 3: Animals that

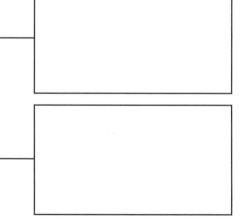

Reproducible   978-1-4129-5336-8 • © Corwin Press

Fantasy Farm

Standard
Life Science—Understand characteristics of organisms.

Strategy
Role play

Objective
Students will distinguish the differences between real-life animals and those presented in fiction.

Materials
Fantasy Farm: Fiction reproducible
Fantasy Farm: Nonfiction reproducible
fiction and nonfiction books about farm animals
chart paper
craft sticks
glue

In this activity, students will learn to distinguish the differences between real-life animals and those presented in fiction. They will come to understand that although animals in storybooks are sometimes endowed with human characteristics, real animals are not.

1. Collect a variety of books about farm animals. Include nonfiction books as well as fictional ones that assign human characteristics to the animals. Choose a nonfiction book to pair with a fiction book each day, and read the two aloud to students.

2. Have students compare how the animals in the two books are presented. Draw a Venn diagram on a sheet of chart paper to record students' observations about each pair of books.

3. When you have finished reading all of the farm books, review the Venn diagrams with students. Then play this simple game. Make a statement about a farm animal, such as: *A dairy cow provides milk* or *A diary cow wears overalls*. Have the students stand up if they think the statement describes a real animal or stay seated if they think it describes a fantasy animal.

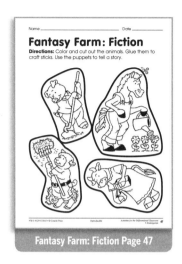

Fantasy Farm: Fiction Page 47

4. Divide the class into mixed-ability groups, and give each group a copy of the **Fantasy Farm: Fiction** and **Fantasy Farm: Nonfiction reproducibles (pages 47–48)**. Have students work together to color and cut out the puppets and glue each puppet to a craft stick. Let students use the puppets to tell fiction and nonfiction stories about the animals. Have each group perform their stories for the class.

Ideas for More Differentiation

Pair an advanced writer with a beginning writer. Have the two collaborate on a farm animal story. Let the advanced writer write the words and the beginning writer draw the pictures for the story.

Name _____   Date _____

Fantasy Farm: Fiction

Directions: Color and cut out the animals. Glue them to craft sticks. Use the puppets to tell a story.

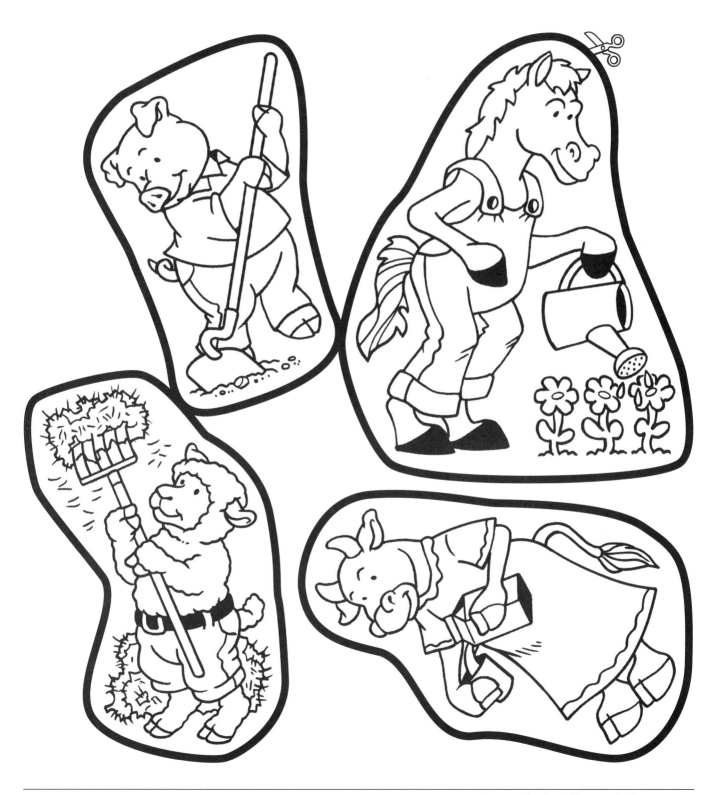

Name _____ Date _____

Fantasy Farm: Nonfiction

Directions: Color and cut out the animals. Glue them to craft sticks. Use the puppets to tell a story.

Reproducible 978-1-4129-5336-8 • © Corwin Press

Mountains of Matches

Standard
Earth Science—Understand properties of earth materials.

Strategy
Center activity

Objective
Students will identify and describe Earth's landforms.

Materials
Mountains of Matches reproducible
spiral-bound calendars
pictures of landforms
writing paper
glue
cardstock

A student's daily experiences expose him or her to a variety of landforms. Depending on where they live, students might see mountains, rivers, lakes, valleys, deserts, or oceans. This activity will help students develop their observation skills, vocabularies, and knowledge of Earth's landforms.

1. Ask parents to donate old calendars that feature photographs of landforms, or download pictures from the Internet. Allow students time to look at all the pictures.

2. Glue sheets of writing paper over the calendar, but leave the photographs uncovered. Allow the glue to dry.

3. To help students focus, select a calendar, and display the photographs one at a time. Invite students to share their observations about each picture. Guide the discussion to include naming the type of landform. Place the remaining calendars in a center, and have students complete the activity or activities appropriate for their level of readiness.

4. **Match the landforms:** Let student pairs play a memory match game. For each student, make one copy of the **Mountains of Matches reproducible (page 51)** on heavy cardstock. Have students color and cut out the pictures. To play the game, students mix up the cards, turn them facedown, and take turns flipping over two cards at a time to find a matching pair. When a match is made, the player who found it keeps the cards and takes another turn.

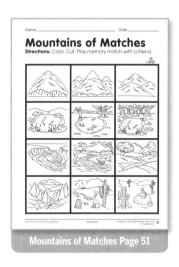

Mountains of Matches Page 51

5. **Name the landform:** Have students work independently to write a sentence telling which landform is pictured.

6. **Characteristics:** Have students list in writing the characteristics of the landform pictured. For example, desert—*dry, hot, dusty, few plants*.

Ideas for More Differentiation

Let students build landform models on a sand-and-water table. Have students identify and name landforms found in your community.

Name _____ Date _____

Mountains of Matches

Directions: Color. Cut. Play memory match with a friend.

Wild Weather

Strategy
Role play

Standard
Earth Science—Understand changes in the earth and sky

Objective
Students will role-play appropriate activities and dress in proper clothing for different weather.

Materials
various articles of clothing for all four seasons

In this activity, students explore how changes in weather affect their lives. Through role play, students note how weather changes with the seasons and describe the different opportunities and limitations that occur with these changes.

1. Prior to the activity, gather various articles of clothing. Ask parents to donate clothing or find thrift store items. You will need to find clothing that would be appropriate for all four seasons. For example, swimsuits and sun hats, sweaters and long pants, mittens and woolly hats, umbrellas and garden gloves.

2. Get students' attention by putting on two unrelated articles of clothing, such as sandals and ski hat. Ask students to tell what the items are and when you would wear them. Have a discussion about the types of clothing that are appropriate for different types of weather. Then talk about how weather effects the types of activities people can do. For example, when there is rain, you can't go swimming, but you can jump in puddles.

3. Divide students into small groups. Give each group various articles of clothing. Instruct students to put the clothing on over their regular clothes. Ask them to create a short skit about an activity children can participate in while wearing the clothing provided. For example, if the group has swimsuits and sun hats, they can act out going to the swimming pool.

4. Bring the whole class back together. Have each group perform their skit in front of the class. Ask the class to guess which season the group demonstrated.

CHAPTER 3

Social Studies

Super Citizens

Standards
Understand the interactions among people, places, and environments.
Understand individual development and identity.

Objective
Students will create a rhyme about proper behavior in the classroom.

Materials
Super Citizens reproducible
chart paper
markers
various books about classroom behavior

Learning cooperation and good citizenship is a key component of the kindergarten curriculum. Students need to discuss proper behavior and analyze the inevitable times when problems arise. In this activity, students will use literature as a vehicle for observing how behavior affects oneself and others.

1. Collect a variety of picture books with a school setting that focus on typical problems young children face. Some good examples are *Lily's Purple Plastic Purse* and *Chrysanthemum* by Kevin Henkes and *Bully, Field Day,* and *Mickey's Class Play* by Judith Caseley.

2. Make a chart on chart paper. Write the name of the main character and how he or she behaved. Then write the solution. For example, *Lily; disrupted class; Mr. Slinger took away her purse; Lily apologized and waited for the right time to share her things.*

3. Select one book to read aloud to students each day. Discuss with students the problems the characters faced and how they dealt with them. Fill in one row of your chart for each book.

4. After you have read all the books to the class, have students create a rhyme. Divide the class into mixed-ability groups. Let each group choose one of the books to read and analyze. Encourage groups to refer to the chart as a reminder.

5. Instruct groups to create a rhyme about the character and his or her behavior. Have them practice several times and then perform for the class.

6. Lead a discussion about good citizenship. Give each student a copy of the **Super Citizens reproducible (page 55)**. Let students fill in the award for someone they believe has demonstrated good citizenship. Distribute the awards, and celebrate proper behavior!

Super Citizens Page 55

Name _____   Date _____

Super Citizens

Directions: Fill out the award. Color it. Cut it out. Give it to a Super Citizen!

Super Citizen Award

Presented to _____

For _____

By _____

Date _____

Treasure Hunt

Strategy
Jigsaw

Standard
Understand the interactions among people, places, and environments. Understand interactions among individuals, groups, and institutions.

Objective
Students will learn about people at their school and what they do.

Materials
Treasure Hunt reproducible
butcher paper
markers
box to act as a treasure chest
small prizes to fill the treasure chest
pirate-themed music
CD or cassette player

In this jigsaw activity, students will have the opportunity to explore the school environment while learning about the work that many people at the school do. They will also begin working with simple maps and learning directional words such as *left, right, near, far,* and so on.

1. Prior to the activity, arrange for several adult volunteers to help you when students are moving around the campus to meet and interact with other staff members. Be sure that each person your students plan to visit knows when they are coming and what to expect. Ask any of the following people to assist you with this project—principal, assistant principal, psychologist, nurse, secretary, librarian, computer technician, food server, janitor, and other teachers.

2. On a large sheet of butcher paper, draw a simple map of your school. Clearly identify places to which a group of students will travel. For example, clearly label the principal's office, the

cafeteria, and the library. Draw the route that students will follow on the map. Mark the last stop with a large X to indicate a treasure. Write the words *Treasure Map* on the part that shows your classroom. Be sure to include your classroom as the starting place of the route.

3. Fill a box with small trinkets for your students—erasers, pencils, stickers, and/or crayons. Hide the box in the classroom.

4. Roll up the treasure map and tie it with string. Display the map prominently in your room to build interest.

5. Read a book that presents the concept of a buried treasure to students, such as *How I Became a Pirate* by Melinda Long. Talk about why someone might bury a treasure and how the treasure would later be found again.

6. Tell students that you found something very interesting in your classroom today. Hold up the rolled treasure map, and ask if anyone knows what it might be. After a few guesses, unroll the map, and show it to the students.

7. Discuss the purpose of the treasure hunt. Tell students they will find out about people who work in the school. Brainstorm a list of appropriate questions to ask the staff members whom students will visit. Assign each student one question to ask throughout the treasure hunt. Remind them to behave appropriately and use good manners while moving around the school.

8. Assign an adult volunteer to lead each treasure hunting group. Divide the class into mixed-ability groups. As volunteers and students walk through the school, have the volunteers point out different features of the campus and ask students to describe what they see and hear. Prompt them to follow the map you provided in the classroom. Encourage the use of directional words such as *left/right*, *near/far*, and so on. When students reach the destination, introduce the staff member to the students, and allow students to ask their questions about the person's job.

9. After groups have collected their information, return to the classroom. Give groups several minutes to organize what they learned about the person they interviewed. Tell them to make sure they know three things about him or her. Encourage the adult volunteer to help the group.

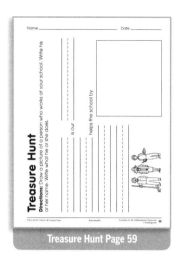

10. Give each student three copies of the **Treasure Hunt reproducible (page 59)**. Have them draw a picture of their interviewee and complete the sentence frames. Play some lively, pirate music. Prompt students to move around the room at random. When the music stops, students find a partner who was not in their treasure hunt group and exchange information about the people they interviewed. Tell them to draw a picture of the other group's person and complete the sentence frames on the second reproducible. Students with developing writing skills can dictate sentences to a volunteer. Repeat the process one more time for the third reproducible.

11. Tell students they can search for the buried treasure once they have reported what they learned about the people in your school. Invite students to tell who they interviewed and what they learned about him or her. Encourage students to talk about the other groups' interviewees, as well. When you feel students have shared all they know, let them find the treasure box. It can be buried in any number of places in the classroom, such as under a pile of books or sports equipment. Distribute the items to students.

Ideas for More Differentiation

For beginning mastery students, photocopy a picture of the staff member they will visit, and attach it to the reproducible. Ask students with a high degree of mastery to write sentences about which professionals might work together or do similar jobs. Ask students to compare the interviewees' jobs with those of other community members.

Treasure Hunt

Directions: Draw a picture of a person who works at your school. Write his or her name. Write what he or she does.

_____

_____ is our

_____

_____ helps the school by

_____

Land, Air, and Sea

Strategy
Rehearsal

Standards

Understand how people organize for the production, distribution, and consumption of goods and services.

Understand relationships among science, technology, and society.

Objective

Students will identify modes of transportation.

Materials

Land, Air, and Sea reproducible
toy vehicles
butcher paper (green or tan, light blue, dark blue)
art supplies

Learning about various modes of transportation is a common theme in kindergarten. In this activity, students will rehearse identifying types of transportation by designing a mural that shows ways of traveling on the land, in the air, and on the sea.

1. Ask parents to donate small toy vehicles, such as cars, trucks, emergency vehicles, boats, airplanes, and so on. Display the vehicles where students can see and touch them.

2. Encourage students to think about vehicles that can be used on the land, in the air, and on the sea, and describe how and where they would be used. Have students sort the collection of toy vehicles into the three categories—land, air, and sea. Ask them to compare the vehicles' features based on the categories.

3. Cover a bulletin board with three different colors of butcher paper. Use green or tan to represent land, dark blue for the sea, and light blue for the air. Title the bulletin board *From Here to There*.

4. Invite students to create a mural about transportation. Give each student a copy of the **Land, Air, and Sea reproducible (page 62)**. Have beginning mastery students color and cut out the pictures. Ask them to say the name of each vehicle and place it in the correct place on the bulletin board. Invite approaching-mastery students to use the illustrations as a model for making their own pictures of vehicles. Have them attach the appropriate sections on the bulletin board. Ask high-degree mastery students to identify the different features of vehicles and what makes them appropriate

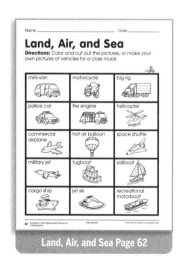

Land, Air, and Sea Page 62

for that type of transportation. For example: *Airplanes have wings so they can fly, but some airplanes have floatation devices so they can land on water.*

Ideas for More Differentiation

Let students color the pictures on the reproducible, cut them out, sort them into categories, and glue them onto a sheet of paper. Have students play a guessing game. One student secretly selects a vehicle and then asks *yes* or *no* questions until someone can guess which vehicle it is.

Land, Air, and Sea

Directions: Color and cut out the pictures, or make your own pictures of vehicles for a class mural.

mini-van	motorcycle	big rig
police car	fire engine	helicopter
commercial airplane	hot air balloon	space shuttle
military jet	tugboat	sailboat
cargo ship	jet ski	recreational motorboat

978-1-4129-5336-8 • © Corwin Press

Job Fair

Standards
Understand the interactions among people, places, and environments.
Understand individual development and identity.

Strategies
Project

Presentation

Objective
Students will teach others about jobs in the community.

Materials
Job Fair, Part 1 reproducible
Job Fair, Part 2 reproducible
various props for community workers
storage boxes

In this activity, students will transform your classroom into a job fair. They will research various community jobs and present their information to classmates. Students will set up booths to teach each other about jobs within the community. This activity gives students the opportunity to examine and use real, professional equipment and to build their knowledge of how people work together within a community.

1. Prior to the activity, assemble a few of the Community Jobs Prop Boxes as indicated below. Borrow props as needed from community workers or parents. Change the professions to reflect some of the jobs common in your area.

   Community Jobs Prop Boxes
   - Doctor—stethoscope, thermometer, blood pressure cuff, tongue depressors, scrubs, scale
   - Restaurant Worker—menu, tablecloth, order pad, apron, pen, dishes, pots, pans, spatulas, oven mitts, cash register
   - Banker—deposit slips, pen, pencil, calculator, rolled coins, dollar bills, loan application, fictitious bank statement
   - Newspaper Reporter—notepad, pen, pencil, microphone, tape recorder, newspaper, dictionary, thesaurus, maps, laptop computer
   - Homemaker—calendar, computer, checkbook, set of keys, cookbook, household items
   - Letter Carrier—mailbag, letters and postcards, shipping boxes, postage stamps, postal scale

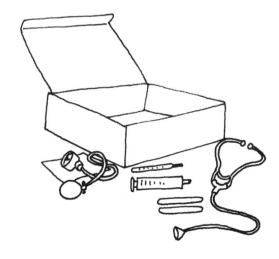

- Police Officer—hat, badge, flashlight, toy handcuffs, megaphone, citation pad
- Firefighter—helmet, gloves, boots, face mask, hose

2. To help students focus, brainstorm with them a list of common community jobs. Have students talk with a partner about jobs with which they are familiar. Then ask volunteers to tell about the jobs their parents do. Write the job titles on the board.

3. Introduce one prop box at a time. Let students examine the props and make guesses about what jobs they represent. After revealing the name of each job, lead a discussion about the duties of someone in that job.

4. Tell students they will ask their parents to help them make a prop box for a classroom job fair. During the fair, the students will present their prop boxes and a poster about the job they chose. Show a sample poster. Make one copy of the **Job Fair, Part 1** and **Job Fair, Part 2 reproducibles (page 65–66)**. Fill in the date of the job fair, and then give each student a copy to take home.

5. Give students about a week to prepare for the job fair. On the day of the fair, set up tables for the students to display their posters and the items from their prop boxes. Allow time for students to explore the displays independently. Then have them walk through the fair together, stopping at each display. The student who created the display will then give a brief description of the job he or she chose.

Job Fair, Part 1 Page 65

Ideas for More Differentiation

Provide an opportunity for willing students to create a commercial about the job fair. Film the commercial, and use it as an invitation for parents and other classes to come and visit the job fair.

Name _____ Date _____

Job Fair, Part 1

Directions: Choose a job. Make a prop box with items used in that job. Make a poster about the job. Use these two pages to plan your project.

My class is having a Job Fair on _____
_ _

_ _

I will talk about _____

Circle what you will do to learn about this job.

Visit the library.	Use a computer.	Read books.

Talk to an expert. 	Watch a TV show about it. 	Visit the place where the job is done. 

Job Fair, Part 2

Directions: Fill in the lines.

_____

- - - - - - - - - - - - - -

1. People with this job do these things: _____

_____

- -

_____

- -

_____

_____

- - - - - - - - - - - - - -

2. People with this job use these things: _____

_____

- -

_____

_____

- - - - - - - - - - - - - -

3. To have a job like this, you have to _____

_____

- -

_____

_____

- -

_____

978-1-4129-5336-8 • © Corwin Press

Our President

Standards
Social Studies—Understand how people create and change structures of power, authority, and governance.
Understand the ideals, principles, and practices of citizenship in a democratic republic.

Strategy
Choice board

Objective
Students will choose an activity to demonstrate their knowledge of the roles of the pPresident of the United States.

Materials
President Choice Board reproducible

Learning about the American presidency helps students connect history with their lives. In this activity, students learn about the role of the president of the United States.

1. Collect portraits of George Washington, Thomas Jefferson, Abraham Lincoln, Franklin Roosevelt, and other presidents from American history. Be sure to include a picture of today's president, as well. To help students activate prior knowledge, display the portraits, and ask students what the people have in common. (*They were all American presidents.*)

2. Explain to students that the president is the leader of our country. Ask students what they think this means. They should realize that the president is primarily responsible for enforcing the laws of the country. Teach students about the role of the American president. Try some of the following:
   - Read books to students about the presidency, such as *Hail to the Chief: The American Presidency* by Don Robb or *The Presidency (A True Book)* by Patricia Quiri.
   - Prepare a virtual tour of the White House using the Internet.
   - Show videos about the office of president.
   - Show pictures of the president engaged in various activities related to the role as leader of the country.

3. Give each student a copy of the **President Choice Board reproducible (page 68)**. Have students select an activity to complete. Allow adequate time for them to prepare, and monitor their progress as necessary. Invite students to present their project to the class.

President Choice Board Page 68

Name _____ Date _____

President Choice Board

Directions: Choose one activity.

Read a book about the president, and report on it. 	Write an acrostic poem about the president. 	Draw a picture of what the president does. 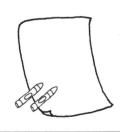
Give a speech as if you were the president. 	Free Choice	Write a song about the president and what he or she does. 
Give a puppet show about something the president does. 	Make a poster about what the president does.	Create a timeline about a famous president. 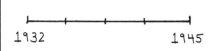

CHAPTER 4

Language Arts

Letter Laundry

Standard

Apply a wide range of strategies to comprehend, interpret, evaluate, and appreciate texts. Draw on prior experience, interactions with other readers and writers, knowledge of word meaning and of other texts, word identification strategies, and understanding of textual features (e.g., sound-letter correspondence, sentence structure, context, graphics).

Objective

Students practice identifying and naming the letters of the alphabet.

Materials

52 white socks
26 clothespins
small laundry basket
string
fabric markers

Strategies
Center activity

Sponge activity

In this activity, students will practice identifying and naming the letters of the alphabet. The activity can be set up as a center, or it can be used as a sponge activity for the whole class when transitional times need to be used productively.

1. Collect 26 pairs of identical white socks. Use a permanent marker to write one uppercase letter from *A* to *Z* on 26 socks and one lowercase letter from *a* to *z* on the remaining 26 socks. Mix up the socks, and put them in a laundry basket.

2. Hang a clothesline (string) over the work area for this activity. Attach 26 clothespins to the line.

3. Tell students that there are three tasks at this center. First, find and name each letter while pinning the sock to the clothesline. Second, find an uppercase letter and its matching lowercase letter, and pin the two socks to the clothesline. Third, create words with the letters and pin the socks to the clothesline.

4. You may choose to let students work individually on this activity, or you may want to have students work in pairs. Encourage students to work at their level of readiness before attempting other tasks at the center.

Ideas for More Differentiation

Have students bring a pair of white socks from home. Assign each student one letter, and have the students make sock puppets of things that begin with their assigned letters. For example, the student who is assigned the letter *Aa* could make puppets of an astronaut and an alligator.

Rhyme Time

Standards

Apply a wide range of strategies to comprehend, interpret, evaluate, and appreciate texts. Draw on prior experience, interactions with other readers and writers, knowledge of word meaning and of other texts, word identification strategies, and understanding of textual features (e.g., sound-letter correspondence, sentence structure, context, graphics).

Apply knowledge of language structure, language conventions (e.g., spelling and punctuation), media techniques, figurative language, and genre to create, critique, and discuss print and nonprint texts.

Objective

Students will say rhyming words.

Materials

Rhyme Time reproducible
soccer ball
marker

Strategies
Focus activity

Preassessment

Using rhyming words is an important way to develop phonemic awareness. In this activity, students play a simple rhyming game as a group and then work with partners to continue practice with rhyming words. Use this activity to assess students' level of readiness for learning or as a focus activity when beginning a unit.

1. Get a black-and-white soccer ball. Use a permanent marker to draw simple pictures and write their names in the white spaces of the ball. Use the **Rhyme Time reproducible (page 73)** as a model for some of the pictures.

2. Have students sit in a circle on the floor. Roll the ball to one student. Tell the student to name the picture that is closest to his or her right thumb. The student then rolls the ball to someone else, and that student names a word that rhymes with the first word. Continue the game by having each student who gets the ball name a word that rhymes with the first word. When no more rhyming words can be named, the student holding the ball starts a new round by naming the picture that is closest to his or her right thumb.

Rhyme Time Page 73

3. After playing several rounds of the game, have students choose partners. Give each pair of students a copy of the **Rhyme Time reproducible (page 73)**. Have students cut out the pictures and put them facedown in a stack. One student draws from the stack, places the picture faceup, and names the picture. Students then take turns offering rhyming words. The last student to name a rhyming word keeps the picture and draws the next card. Play continues until all of the pictures have been turned over. The winner of the game is the student who has collected the most pictures.

Ideas for More Differentiation

For students who are ready, list the rhyming words on chart paper. Point out how the beginning sound and letter changes, but the ending sound and letters stay the same.

Rhyme Time

Directions: Cut out the cards. Play a game with a partner. Listen to your teacher for directions.

cat	hand	snail
ten	bed	feet
pig	slide	five
clock	frog	boat
drum	sun	skunk

Sing Along with Letters

Strategy
Rehearsal

Standard

Apply a wide range of strategies to comprehend, interpret, evaluate, and appreciate texts. Draw on prior experience, interactions with other readers and writers, knowledge of word meaning and of other texts, word identification strategies, and understanding of textual features (e.g., sound-letter correspondence, sentence structure, context, graphics).

Objective

Students will practice beginning sounds of words.

Materials

Beginning Sounds reproducible
scissors

In this activity, students will learn a simple song to practice the sounds of beginning consonants. Carefully select the order in which letters are introduced. Letter sounds that are easily confused, such as /b/ and /p/, should be separated in the sequence of instruction.

1. For each new beginning consonant sound you introduce, have students bring in one item from home that begins with that sound. Display the items, and have students name each item to practice saying the sound.

2. Teach students this simple song, sung to the tune of "Mary Had a Little Lamb":
   The letter *b* says
   /b/, /b/, /b/,
   /b/, /b/, /b/,
   /b/, /b/, /b/.
   The letter *b* says /b/, /b/, /b/,
   Like *big* and *bet* and *bug*.
   Substitute the letter name, sound, and three simple words for each new letter.

3. Make a copy of the **Beginning Sounds reproducible (page 76)**. Write a consonant in the box on the Word Finder and a word ending in each box on the Word Strip. Make a copy for each student. Have the students cut out the shapes, cut slits on the dotted lines, and thread the Word Strip through the slits. Then have students pull the Word Strip through the Word Finder, reading each word as it appears.

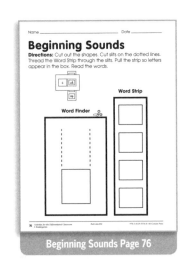

Beginning Sounds Page 76

Ideas for More Differentiation

Provide visual learners with ready-to-be-recycled magazines, and have them cut out pictures of things that begin with a given letter. Ask them to create a collage of pictures and show their work to the group. Challenge students with a high degree of mastery to create a song using ending sounds.

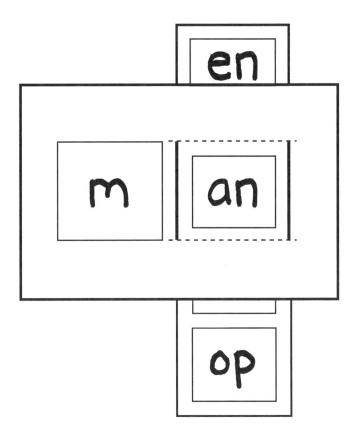

Beginning Sounds

Directions: Cut out the shapes. Cut slits on the dotted lines. Thread the Word Strip through the slits. Pull the strip so letters appear in the box. Read the words.

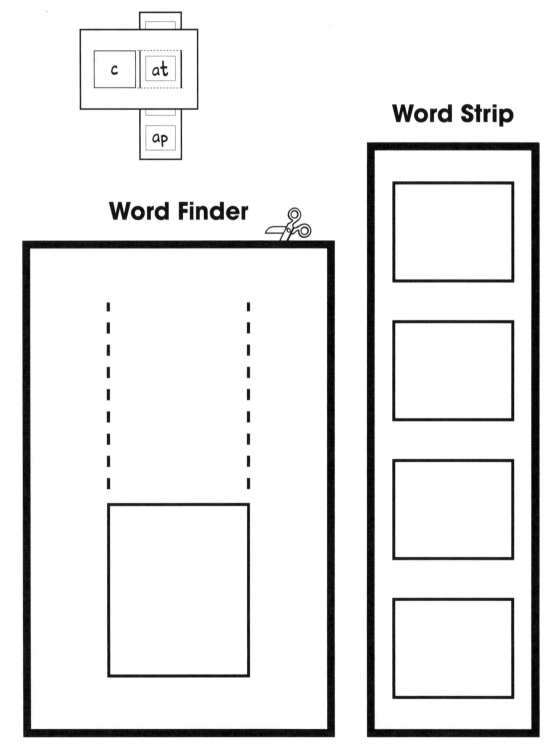

Word Strip

Word Finder

978-1-4129-5336-8 • © Corwin Press

What Do You Hear?

Standard

Apply a wide range of strategies to comprehend, interpret, evaluate, and appreciate texts. Draw on prior experience, interactions with other readers and writers, knowledge of word meaning and of other texts, word identification strategies, and understanding of textual features (e.g., sound-letter correspondence, sentence structure, context, graphics).

Objective

Students will match letters to sounds.

Materials

What Do You Hear? reproducible
flannel board
lowercase flannel letters

Strategies
Preassessment

Rehearsal

Matching sounds to letters is an important first step in learning to decode words. In this activity, you will read words to students, and they will identify the sounds they hear. This activity is great as a preassessment to determine students' level of readiness for learning phonics. Or, use this activity as a rehearsal by working with small groups of students who need more practice.

1. Display the flannel letters a few at a time on a flannel board. Have students review the letter names and corresponding sounds.

2. Say a few simple words such as *cat, ball,* and *sand*. For each word, have a different student identify the beginning sound by placing the appropriate letter on the flannel board. Say more words, but this time have students identify the ending sounds. Finally, say one more set of words with short-vowel sounds in the middle, and have students identify the vowels.

3. Give each student a copy of the **What Do You Hear? reproducible (page 79)**. Read aloud the following list of words. For words 1–4, students circle the beginning sounds; words 5–8, they circle the ending sounds; and words 9–12, they circle the middle sounds.

What Do You Hear? Page 79

1. fun

2. puppet

3. me

4. car

5. not

6. her

7. small

8. pig

9. hop

10. did

11. can

12. red

Ideas for More Differentiation

Have students write the letter sounds they hear in the words you read. Choose one word, such as *plant*, and have students write it vertically on a piece of paper. Then have them write one word for each letter within the original word. For example: *p—pup, l—let, a—ant, n—net, t—top*.

What Do You Hear?

Directions: Listen to your teacher. Circle the letter you hear at the beginning of the word.

1. m   g   f   **2.** p   t   b

3. m   k   d   **4.** l   c   w

Directions: Listen to your teacher. Circle the letter you hear at the end of the word.

5. t   q   a   **6.** y   r   b

7. l   h   p   **8.** g   s   i

Directions: Listen to your teacher. Circle the letter you hear in the middle of the word.

9. z   t   o   **10.** u   i   v

11. a   m   e   **12.** e   x   o

Mega Matches

Standard
Apply a wide range of strategies to comprehend, interpret, evaluate, and appreciate texts. Draw on prior experience, interactions with other readers and writers, knowledge of word meaning and of other texts, word identification strategies, and understanding of textual features (e.g., sound-letter correspondence, sentence structure, context, graphics).

Objective
Students match letters or words with pictures of words.

Materials
Mega Match 1 reproducible
Mega Match 2 reproducible
butcher paper
magazines or catalogs
scissors
pushpins
string
sentence strips
masking tape
stapler

In this activity, students practice reading words and matching them to pictures. Students will work in pairs at the center.

1. Cover a bulletin board with butcher paper, and title the board *Mega Matches*. This bulletin board will serve as a reading center.

2. Gather ready-to-be-recycled magazines and catalogs. Find pictures that represent simple one-syllable, two-syllable, and three-syllable words, and cut them out. Laminate the pictures, and staple them in rows on the bulletin board.

3. Write the letters and words that go with the pictures on pieces of sentence strips. Staple the letters and words in rows opposite the pictures so the rows are about 12 inches apart.

4. Cut a 24-inch length of yarn for each letter or word and picture pair. Staple one end of each length of yarn beneath a picture. Let the other end hang free. Wrap the free end in masking tape. Put a pushpin above each word.

5. Have students visit the center individually or in pairs. Let them study the pictures and read the letters and words. Then have them pin the yarn to the matching word. Beginning mastery students can match letters to initial sounds of the word pictured. Approaching mastery students can match one-syllable words to pictures. Challenge students with a high degree of mastery to match two- or three-syllable words to pictures.

6. Let students choose partners to play a memory match game. Give each pair of students a copy of the **Mega Match 1** and **Mega Match 2 reproducibles (pages 82–83)** to play the game. The players cut out the cards, mix them up, and place them facedown in rows. Each player takes a turn flipping over two cards to make a match. If a match is made, that player takes another turn. If not, play shifts to the other player. The game is over when all of the matches have been found. The student with the most matches wins.

Ideas for More Differentiation

Provide more practice for beginning mastery students. Make a copy of page 82, and cut out the cards. Make a set of self-correcting flashcards by gluing each word to one side of an index card and the picture to the other side. Students can practice reading the words and checking their own answers.

Mega Match 1 Page 82

Mega Match 1

Directions: Cut out the cards. Play Memory Match with a friend.

		crab	**fan**
shell	**tent**	**chick**	**sink**
sock	**mop**	**truck**	**mug**

Reproducible

978-1-4129-5336-8 • © Corwin Press

Mega Match 2

Directions: Cut out the cards. Play Memory Match with a friend.

the	the	of	of
and	and	a	a
to	to	in	in
is	is	you	you
that	that	it	it

In the Clouds

Standards

Apply a wide range of strategies to comprehend, interpret, evaluate, and appreciate texts. Draw on prior experience, interactions with other readers and writers, knowledge of word meaning and of other texts, word identification strategies, and understanding of textual features (e.g., sound-letter correspondence, sentence structure, context, graphics).

Adjust use of spoken, written, and visual language (e.g., conventions, style, vocabulary) to communicate effectively with a variety of audiences and for different purposes.

Apply knowledge of language structure, language conventions (e.g., spelling and punctuation), media techniques, figurative language, and genre to create, critique, and discuss print and nonprint texts.

Objective

Students will build their vocabularies by categorizing words.

Materials

In the Clouds reproducible
sidewalk chalk
chart paper
markers
game markers

Students will build their vocabularies with this activity. They will brainstorm words that fit into given categories and practice writing words that that can be categorized together.

1. Divide your class into three teams. Take the teams outside. Use sidewalk chalk to draw a row of four boxes about the size of hopscotch boxes for each team.

2. Write the name of a category in each box. Use different categories for each team. For example: *weather, songs, zoo animals, foods, sports, books, places, TV characters, colors, musical instruments, clothing,* and *farm animals*.

3. Have the teams line up an equal distance away from their boxes. Have the first student in each line toss a game marker onto the team's boxes. He or she then names a word that belongs to the category in the box where the marker lands. If possible, have the student write the word in the box. The next player in line then takes a turn.

4. Record each student's responses on a sheet of chart paper designated for each team. Play continues until one team has at least four words recorded for each of its four categories.

5. When you return to the classroom, give each student a copy of the **In the Clouds reproducible (page 86)**. Have students write the name of a category in the sun and a word that belongs to that category on each cloud.

Ideas for More Differentiation

Hang the sheets of chart paper around the room. Encourage students with a high degree of mastery to write stories using the words. Have other students take words from one category and sort them into even smaller groups. For example, the broad category of *food* can be sorted into *fruits and vegetables, meats, dairy, grains,* and *sweets.*

In the Clouds Page 86

Name _____ Date _____

In the Clouds

Directions: Write the name of a category on the sun. Write a word that goes with the category on each cloud.

978-1-4129-5336-8 • © Corwin Press

Donut Details

Standards

Read a wide range of print and nonprint texts to build an understanding of texts, of self, and of the cultures of the United States and the world; to acquire new information; to respond to the needs and demands of society and the workplace; and for personal fulfillment (includes fiction and nonfiction, classic, and contemporary works).

Read a wide range of literature from many periods in many genres to build an understanding of the many dimensions (e.g., philosophical, ethical, aesthetic) of human experience.

Objective

Students will use a graphic organizer to compare themselves to characters they have read about.

Materials

Donut Details reproducible
chart paper
markers
read-aloud book

Students who can connect their personal experiences with those they read about will have a greater ability to comprehend what they read. In this activity, students will use a graphic organizer to compare themselves to characters they have read about. Use this activity with the whole class or with small groups.

1. Select a picture book to read aloud to students. Point out the features of the book, including the cover, title page, dedication, and summary on the back cover or dust jacket.

2. As you read, ask students to summarize the main events of the story every few pages.

3. When you finish reading the book, ask students who the story was mostly about. Invite them to describe interesting things about the main character, and write their responses on a sheet of chart paper.

4. Ask students to tell how they are different from the main character and how they are similar. List these responses on another sheet of chart paper.

978-1-4129-5336-8

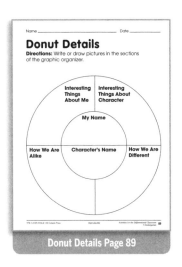

Donut Details Page 89

5. Hang the charts that you made in a place where students can see them. Give each student a copy of the **Donut Details reproducible (page 89)**. Have students fill in the graphic organizer with lists of interesting things about themselves and the character and how they are similar to and different from the character. Encourage students to draw pictures to accompany their lists. Model how to complete the Donut Details graphic organizer. Start by showing students where to write their name and the character's name. Then show them how to write or draw pictures about themselves and the character. Finally, demonstrate how to make a comparison at the bottom of the circle.

Donut Details

Directions: Write or draw pictures in the sections of the graphic organizer.

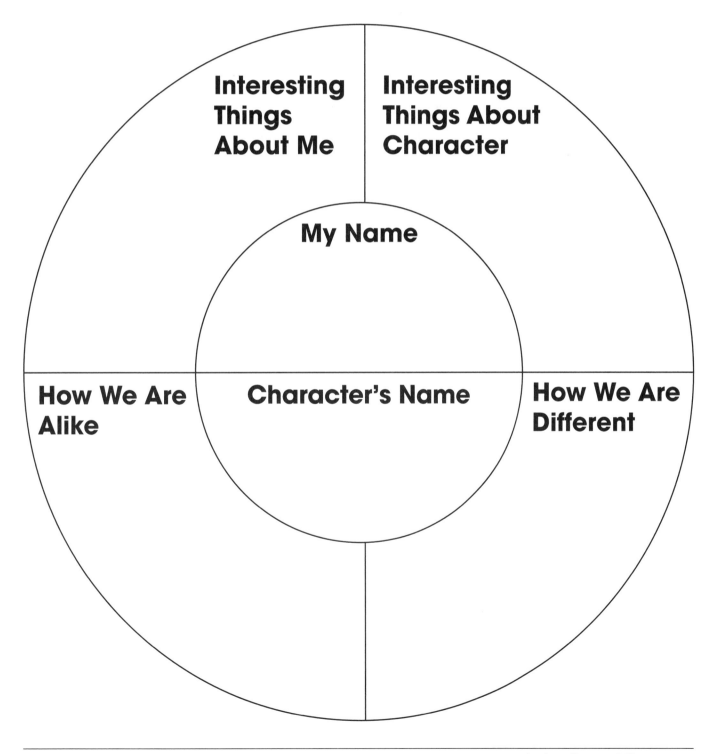

A Picture Says a Thousand Words

Strategy

Cooperative group learning

Standards

Adjust the use of spoken, written, and visual language (e.g., conventions, style, vocabulary) to communicate effectively with a variety of audiences and for different purposes.

Employ a wide range of strategies while writing, and use different writing process elements appropriately to communicate with different audiences for a variety of purposes.

Apply knowledge of language structure, language conventions (e.g., spelling and punctuation), media techniques, figurative language, and genre to create, critique, and discuss print and nonprint texts.

Objective

Students will use wordless picture books to tell a story.

Materials

wordless picture books
sticky notes of various sizes

Studying wordless picture books and creating text for them provides students with a way to tell and write stories. In this activity, students discover they can create quite different stories from the same pictures.

1. Gather a collection of wordless picture books. Suggestions include *Pancakes for Breakfast* by Tomie dePaola, *The Red Book* by Barbara Lehman, *The Snowman* by Raymond Briggs, and *Sidewalk Circus* by Paul Fleischman and Kevin Hawkes.

2. Introduce the books one at a time. Silently display the pictures. Let students study the illustrations and draw their own conclusions about the characters, setting, and plot.

3. Flip through the pages of the book again, but this time, have students describe what is happening in each scene.

4. Divide the class into mixed-ability groups. Let each group choose a book. Tell students they will work together to write the book's story. Give each group pads of different-sized sticky notes. Have them write both narrative text and dialogue on the notes and stick them to the pages in the appropriate places.

5. Have a parent volunteer type up the stories. Let each group present its version of the story to the class. Guide a discussion about how the pictures helped them write the story.

6. To extend the activity, have the groups trade books. Continue until each group has written a story for each of the picture books. Read aloud and compare the different versions of the same story.

Ideas for More Differentiation

Have students with a high degree of mastery create their own picture books with stories. Invite beginning mastery students to tell their stories into a tape recorder or act out the stories.

CHAPTER 5

Physical Education and the Arts

Rollicking Races

Strategy
Rehearsal

Objective

Students will experiment with different movements and practice controlling their bodies as they participate in team races.

Materials

plastic cones

In kindergarten, students find pure enjoyment in just moving their bodies through space. In this activity, students will experiment with different movements and practice controlling their bodies as they participate in team races.

1. Divide students into two teams. Have the teams line up outside in single-file lines. Place a plastic cone several yards away from each team.

2. Tell students that you will call out an animal and the first person in each line will move like that animal to get from the line to the cone and back. The next person in line has to use the same movements as the first. The race continues until each team member has copied the movements.

3. Present enough animals so that each student has a chance to create a specific movement for others to follow. Be sure to use a variety of animals so students can engage in many different types of movements, such as creeping, crawling, hopping, galloping, swaying, walking, and running.

Lots of Lines

Strategies

Preassessment

Rehearsal

Postassessment

Objective

Students will identify types of lines and use correct terminology when describing them.

Materials

easels

paints

painting paper

In this activity, students will experiment with different elements of art, focusing primarily on lines and colors. They will also use the words *vertical, horizontal,* and *diagonal.* This activity allows students to practice their speaking skills while telling classmates about their work.

1. Have your students sit on the floor in front of an easel. Ask them to describe different types of lines—straight, wavy, curly, diagonal, spiral, and so on. Use this opportunity to introduce vocabulary words such as *vertical, horizontal,* and *diagonal.*

2. Invite students to come up to the easel and paint an example of a type of line. You can let students choose what type of line to paint or provide them with various options. Encourage them to use the new vocabulary words.

3. Ask students to tell you what types of lines might be used to depict certain scenes. For example, a painting of a hillside might use wavy lines for the hills and cross-hatched lines for the grass covering the hills.

4. Tell students they will use different colors to paint examples of lines. Provide an easel as well as a variety of paintbrushes and different colors of paint.

5. Invite volunteers to present their paintings to the class and tell about the lines and colors they used. Remind them to use the correct terminology when referring to direction and types of lines.

A Musical Review

Strategy
Choice board

Objective
Students will learn patriotic songs and their histories.

Materials
Music Choice Board reproducible
lyrics for patriotic songs
chart paper
art supplies
musical instruments

Combine a social studies lesson with music by teaching students some patriotic songs. Help them understand the history behind the songs and why they remain important to our country today.

1. Collect the lyrics from several patriotic songs, such as "The Star-Spangled Banner," "You're a Grand Old Flag," "God Bless America," "Battle Hymn of the Republic," "America (My Country 'tis of Thee)," and "America the Beautiful." Print the lyrics on sheets of chart paper.

2. Teach students to sing the songs. Practice for a few minutes each day until students have memorized the songs.

3. As students are learning the songs, give brief history lessons about why the songs were written. For example, Francis Scott Key wrote "The Star-Spangled Banner" when he saw the flag still standing over Fort McHenry after a battle had been fought there.

4. Discuss how patriotic music is used today. Songs are often played during special ceremonies or celebrations and are intended to remind people they are proud of their country.

5. Present students with the **Music Choice Board (page 95)**. Have each student choose the task they would like to do. Provide art supplies for students who make the props or the background. Have musical instruments available for students who will play them in the show. Help students who want to make puppets and act out the songs.

6. Invite parents to come to a musical review in which students perform the songs. If you wish, have one student give a brief introduction to each song, explaining its role in history.

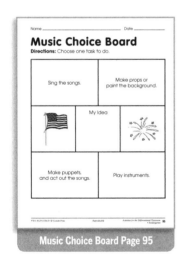

Music Choice Board Page 95

Name _____ Date _____

Music Choice Board

Directions: Choose one task to do.

Sing the songs.	Make props or paint the background.

	My Idea	

Make puppets, and act out the songs.	Play instruments.

References

California Department of Education. (2005). *History-social science sramework for California public schools: Kindergarten through grade 12.* Sacramento, CA: California Department of Education.

California Department of Education. (2006). *Mathematics framework for California public schools: Kindergarten through grade 12.* Sacramento, CA: California Department of Education.

California Department of Education. (1994). *Physical educationframework for California public schools: Kindergarten through grade 12.* Sacramento, CA: California Department of Education.

California Department of Education. (1999). *Reading/language arts framework for California public school: Kindergarten through grade 12.* Sacramento, CA: California Department of Education.

California Department of Education. (2004). *Science framework for California public schools: Kindergarten through grade 12.* Sacramento, CA: California Department of Education.

California Department of Education. (2004). *Visual and performing arts framework for California public schools: Kindergarten through grade 12.* Sacramento, CA: California Department of Education.

Gregory, G. H. & Chapman, C. (2002). *Differentiated instructional strategies: One size doesn't fit all* (2nd ed.). Thousand Oaks, CA: Corwin Press.

National Council for the Social Studies. (2002). *Expectations of excellence: Curriculum standards for social studies.* Silver Spring, MD: National Council for the Social Studies (NCSS).

National Council of Teachers of English and the International Reading Association. (1996). *Standards for the English language arts.* Urbana, IL: National Council of Teachers of English (NCTE).

National Council of Teachers of Mathematics. (2005). *Principles and standards for school mathematics.* Reston, VA: National Council of Teachers of Mathematics (NCTM).

National Research Council. (1996). *National science education standards.* Washington, D.C.: National Academy Press.